THE GATE

OTHER POETRY BY ANN MARIE GEAREN

Homecoming

THE GATE

Poems by

Ann Marie Gearen

Antrim House
Bloomfield, Connecticut

Library of Congress Control Number: 2020938445

ISBN: 978-1-943826-70-4

First Edition, 2020

Printed & bound in the USA

Book design by Rennie McQuilkin

The front cover painting, "Hope Town Burial Society,"
is by Brigitte Bowyer Carey.

Author photograph by John Gearen

Antrim House
860.217.0023
AntrimHouseBooks@gmail.com
www.AntrimHouseBooks.com
400 Seabury Dr., #5196, Bloomfield, CT 06002

For John

ACKNOWLEDGMENTS

Grateful acknowledgment to the editors of the following publications in which these poems first appeared, at times in earlier versions:

Abaco Life, spring 2018: "A Quiet Man"
After Hours: "Anniversary, Uxmal"
After Hours, Issue No. 20-21: "Cancer Dreams"
After Hours, Issue No. 24: "Advice"
After Hours, Issue No. 32-33: "To Wu Dong, from Her Mother in America"
After Hours: "Scarves for My Daughter"
Calyx, Vol 28, No. 1: "Resentment of the Dead Toward the Living"

GRATITUDE

I have been enormously lucky to spend four residencies at Ragdale, an artists' colony in Lake Forest, Illinois. I have written and revised many of these poems there, and I have spent happy, creative hours walking the miles of prairie that surround this magical place. The rooms are said to be haunted, but I have found them haunted only by the muse of poetry. There can be no better place to find enough solitude to work and enough community to learn from other artists.

Thanks to Al De Genova for his work on behalf of poetry in Chicago, from his editing of the literary magazine *After Hours*, now in its 20th year, to his organizing and hosting The Traveling Mollys, a reading series which takes place monthly in downtown or west side bars and cafes. I appreciate his publishing a number of my poems over the years.

I am also most grateful to the members of the Writers' Circle, which has met weekly for over twenty years during the winter months when we are in Hope Town, Abaco, Bahamas, a tiny island which appears often in these poems. The group has been open to all who are willing to share their work each week. At the end of the winter the group has put together a performance, free and open to everyone on the island or on neighboring islands. We have read each year to an enthusiastic full house at the Hope Town Harbour Lodge. The Circle has been a good place to make something new and then to learn from other writers how to make it better.

Among the members of that community, I am particularly indebted to my husband John, to Kate Oakes, and to Doug Hyde. Both my husband and Doug have read the whole manuscript and have offered their astute suggestions. I am hoping the Circle will survive after the devastation caused by Hurricane Dorian.

I owe a debt of gratitude to my children and in-law children for their love and support, and in many cases for their suggestions on individual poems or on the book as a whole.

I could not have imagined an editor and publisher as perfect and as much fun as Rennie McQuilkin. He is as talented and encouraging as he is professional and insightful. With a sure hand, he shepherded these poems into a book in a surprisingly short amount of time. Rennie, I thank you.

My most heartfelt and lasting thanks and boundless love belong to my husband and fellow poet for his support of me throughout this work and all of our lives together. Our ongoing, life-giving forty-five-year conversation has helped make me who I am as a person and as a writer. Thank you, John, for all of it.

TABLE OF CONTENTS

I.

II,

III.

O, what is life but a mouthful of air
Yet all the lovely things that were
Live for I saw them dancing there.

W. B. Yeats

THE GATE

I.

All Saints

All Hallow's Eve has passed.
Leopards, tigers, Raggedy Ann,
the tin man
have taken their candy stash
and trundled it home.

I tuck them in.
Costumes tangled on the floor,
they sleep as themselves,
not goblins,
eyes closed, mouths slightly ajar,
breathing slowed to sighs,
dreaming whatever children dream.

After midnight as Halloween
becomes All Saints' Day
and as I too drift off to sleep,
my beloved dead come
crowding up the stairway of my mind,
the daytime veil between us blown away.

I dream back the laughter, the games of Clue,
Canasta, bingo. In my dream,
I am a girl again, gathering eggs
from my grandmother's chicken coop,
her cherry cobbblers
set to cool on the windowsill,
then watching her can tomatoes in jars
which she sets up like jewels
winking in the darkness
of the musty basement.

Welcome, my saints.
I have missed you all.

The Gate

I have supped with ghosts
sat down with them
risen with them
walked the beach with them
slept beside them
caught a glimpse of them
behind me in the mirror
as I brushed my hair.

Some are as familiar
as the soup on my kitchen stove.
Some are querulous.
What were you thinking? one asks.
I cannot answer.
I don't know myself.
Some are chattering, scolding ghosts.

Sometimes there are several ghosts at once,
part of a group that once gathered
but gathers no more in this world,
although their conversation cheers me,
floats around my head like butterflies or bees.

Some, like the ghost of my mother,
come just when needed
without my calling.
She stays for a few minutes
and then is gone.

The gate
between the living and the dead,
on well-oiled hinges,
swings open as well as shut.

Resentment of the Dead Toward the Living

When my husband's younger sister,
mild as the moon,
was told her cancer
had returned,

I found her in her kitchen
working for hours
in a sweating rage.
The air smelled of cardamom
cinnamon and sage
as she hurled into the trash
with small explosions of glass
spices already expired or
likely to expire
before she would.

Same kitchen, later date.
She is frailer,
her skin almost transparent.
Through her bay window
winter light falls aslant
lights up the crumbs from lunch
still on the table.

How did she feel
watching her young children
sitting in the laps of their aunts,
snuggling with the women
who would help care for them
when she no longer could,
who would see them grow up,
go to college,

graduate, live in Chicago,
New York, China,
marry,
have children.

Years after her death,
she came to me in a dream.
She was driving her car,
with my husband beside her.
I sat behind her, chatting
to her silent back.
I looked at her soft brown curls
and thought, with gratitude,
She is all right. She is OK.

While I talked, she was mute.
When she turned her face to me,
her smile was cruel.
I saw in her eyes –
She doesn't want to be dead alone.

She turned back to face the road,
pulled the wheel hard
to the left, swerving
into the oncoming car
head on.

Sight/Insight

When my mother was diagnosed
with macular degeneration,
I entered her in a clinical trial,
double blind, gold standard.
For a year I drove her
to the hospital
an hour each way
through snow storms or
spring rains.
Alzheimers intervened, but I would not stop.
I wanted her to see.
All her life she had been able to focus on
whatever beauty or good was in her line of sight.

Seeing rainbows around lights
is a symptom.
As we drove home from the hospital
in the winter dark, she would say,
"Look at the rainbows around the car lights, babe!
Can you see them? They're so beautiful!"

We never knew
if she got the medication
or the placebo.

Elegy for a Cellist

For Paula

When my father died,
I danced the tango,
dreaming of a mango-scented breeze,
hot music from Argentina.
Not because I wasn't sad, but
he was a musician
and I am a musician's daughter.

Death has come
to his hands,
age-speckled,
formed to hold his bow,
empty now on the coverlet,

big hands stretched
almost to breaking
with the cello singing,
soaring, answering,
deep and high.

Even as a child,
I watched him onstage,
beautiful in his tuxedo.
Seated in a velvet chair,
I was his audience.
When everyone clapped,
they stood and opened their mouths:
Bravo!

At home
I watched him
listening to music
only he could hear,
strong fingers tapping out a rhythm
on the tablecloth.

Now I see him
playing his cello
in the open air
beside Maine's
Union River Bay,
his form exact,
a breeze barely lifting his white hair,
his focus perfect,
face rapt,
shoulders swaying slightly,
music rising
into a cloudless sky.

Man on a Wire

Seven of his family have died
walking the high wire.
He denies fear:
I am alive on the wire.
All else is only waiting.

If he slipped
he would drop like a missile
to the street below.

Six hundred feet up
above the Chicago River,
wires stretch taut
between two skyscrapers.
He steps off into the night,
into a howling wind,
without a harness,
without a net.

We crane our necks,
hold our collective breath.

He reaches the other side,
then raises his arms in triumph.
From the street
he looks small as a bird.
What relief to see his upraised arms.

He walks the second walk,
back to his starting place,
blindfolded,

prehensile toes in special shoes
made by his mother,
sealed with a prayer.

Before he walks
she blesses him, signs the cross
over him. He believes
angels hold him aloft.

We all walk a wire
we do not see,
death beside us, death below us.

We do not feel the wire beneath our feet
in this precious, precarious world.

Celebrating a Birth

for Valentina

To celebrate a new baby
whose belly is round as the Buddha's,
whose smile is warm as the Dalai Lama's,
I have given flowers for the altar
of our little church,
daffodils, freesia, ranunculus.

It is not enough.
I want more.

If I were in Mumbai
during the festival of the
elephant god Ganesh,
I would wear a red silk sari,
feel its swish against my ankles.
Bedecked with gold,
ankle bracelet jangling,
red sari swirling,
I would join the crowds
dancing in the streets
full of color, movement
and the smell of incense,
lifting up prayers to Ganesh,
Ganesh, remover of obstacles,

for obstacles were thrust aside
so she could be born.

All dancers would head toward the sea

where I would raise his statue
draped with necklaces of marigolds,
hold it over my head as I wade into the lapping ocean,
sari dragging, heavy now with water,
and set the god free upon the waters
to join the thousands of other images
brought by other worshipers, all
saying silently, *Thank you, thank you, Ganesh.*

To Wu Dong, from Her Mother in America

for Iris

Wu Dong, Bright East, today
I received glad news that you are mine.
In the photo they sent
your face is grave.
Someone is holding you up
in your quilted jacket.
They are not visible
except for their hands.

I am sad I cannot come to you.
People in your province have fallen ill
with an unknown sickness.
The streets are nearly empty.
Families stay inside in fear,
spending their days watching
from the windows.

Every day more small caskets
are carried to cemeteries.
Wearing white for mourning,
mothers and fathers
are wailing.
They are burning paper money
so their child will want for nothing
in the next life. Ashes float
in the yellow air.

If this sickness were a dragon,
I would come with my sword

and kill it.
If your house were on fire,
I would hold you and jump
through the flames.
If the sickness were a flood,
I would come in my flat-bottomed boat
and pole you through the rapids
to safety, with you in that quilted jacket
lying flat on your back,
staring calmly at the rainy sky.

Cancer Dreams

Waking, I ask,
Was it something I did, or
something I failed to do?

In one dream, it seems
I've forgotten something
important, for which
I will be severely punished.

In another dream, I'm underwater,
trapped in whitewater current,
canoe overturned
wedged against a rock,
my foot caught in a strap.
I cannot surface.

In a third, dogs leap at me,
rending flesh.
Then I'm alone
in a dark wood
running, panicked
until I arrive
at the point where I began.

Was it something I ate
or didn't eat?
Something in the water, the air?
Did I raise my daughters in a poisoned place?

And these others, the morning patients
in the oncology radiation waiting room –
what did they do? We exchange glances,

measure ourselves against the prognosis
we see in each other. We offer tips:
use aloe on the burn,
no underwire in the bra.

In a silent room
I await results from a test
that will show if my cancer
is something I could have passed on
to my older daughter,
already stricken as I am,
or to my younger daughter.
"No," she says, "this is not hereditary.
It is chance."

Then the doctor recites my options,
the trade-offs and bad bargains:
so many weeks of burning,
a small Nagasaki,
for certain years, or months
more of life,
five years of hormonal side effects
for a four percent better chance
of survival.

Oh, to be a steer, and
not see it coming,
prodded up a wooden walkway.
One moment of fear, eyes rolling,
then a quick blow to the head, and
fear and life are ended.

Later, when I am polishing
my grandmother's silver pitcher,

making the tarnish give way to shine –
a place on the handle is worn down to
tin by the hands of four generations
of women who polished and poured –
I summon my grandmother,
almost a hundred when she died, and
my mother, almost eighty-eight
when she died from Alzheimers,
not cancer.

Polishing this pitcher tells me
in my muscles, my hands,
that despite my fears,
good things too
may be passed down, passed along.

Nothing is as cold and sweet
as icy water
poured from a silver pitcher.

Scarves for My Daughter

for Cameron

After fingering the printed silk,
pre-tied, gathered to stay on a slippery head,
I choose a purple cloche,
then a hand-knit hat in rose and
a light blue cotton sleeping cap,
to warm the sleeping head
of my soon-to-be-bald daughter.

I hand my credit card
to the "image specialist"
who points out barber chairs
where she performs buzz cuts.
"Better to be pro-active,"
she says, "and not wait to
watch your hair hit the shower drain."
My daughter's hair should be
leaving her next week.
Her eyebrows and lashes
may soon follow.

As a baby, she was late
to have hair at all.
When it grew in at last,
it was white blond, and so
fine she still looked nearly bald.

I had to tape a red bow
to her head for her formal baby portrait
just to show she was a girl.

Death of a Brave Man

for Beth

Considerate to a fault,
he bore his suffering
as he was able,
through night and day,
through the darkness
which never goes away,
despite the love in the eyes of
those he loved,
despite the famous doctor,
the newest pills,
the newest combinations of pills,
which he took
despite their side effects:
weight gain, memory loss.

With long and careful planning
he bought insurance
which would pay the family
of a suicide, but only
if it took place
at least one year
from date of purchase.

He waited. He became a statue.
His eyes turned to stone,
each day's survival near heroic.
He lay in bed for hours, unable
to sit up, to turn over,
unable to lift his head.

Finally, on the appointed day,
he rose from his bed
to complete his last task.

With what relief, near joy,
he cleaned and vacuumed his car,
returned his overdue library books.
With what sadness
he kissed his children,
left a note: *(Dear Ones,*
All my failures are mine alone),
drove to an out of the way motel
his family could not know,
and accurately, finally,
put a bullet through his brain.

Last Light

Your eyes are closed.
Your breathing slows,
long pauses in between.

Your skin hangs on your frame,
but the brain, that huge computer,
stuffed with memory, judgment, humor . . .

I watch it close up shop
as the fire behind your eyes is banked,
as your one last light goes out.

II.

Hope Town Burial Society

Entering the soft half-darkness
of the small clapboard building
of the Hope Town Burial Society,
I'm struck by the tang of fresh cut pine.
Wood shavings litter the floor.
Winer Malone's plane
shaped and smoothed
the two coffins there:
one ready now,
one in reserve.

They used to keep a
child-sized coffin,
but with good doctors and better medicine,
there is no longer a need. Years ago,
the last small one
was used for Aunt Vernie,
a tiny woman who just fit.

At the Society's annual meeting,
we have come to join, along with our neighbors.
We sit in the well-worn pews of St. James
bowing our heads
as Miss Suzanne opens the meeting with a prayer:
"God of love, may we be of use to others
as they face sad times in their lives."

On this small island,
cemeteries are almost full. The agenda:
find new burial land.

One member asks if neighbors will object to
having a graveyard next door.
Miss Shelley points out
the dead make good neighbors.

We pay our yearly dues,
a bargain at twenty dollars apiece
covering funeral, coffin and burial.

When we must leave this world,
how good it would be to leave
in a ship of death made by Winer Malone,
master boat builder whose hand
built graceful wooden Abaco dinghies
still sailing these blue green waters.

There will be no frills,
just the familiar smell of pine
as a body is committed
to this soil of sand and coral.

Meeting adjourned,
we all walk out into warm night air
under a sky hung close with stars.

Someone laughs, saying
"And the best thing is
you never pay for your own funeral!"

A Quiet Man

Winer Malone, November 1, 1929 – January 21, 2018

Miss Margaret told me
that Mr. Winer Malone
had passed last night.
Passed seemed the right word,
as he used to pass through the settlement
like a benign ghost.
I would not have been surprised
to see him walk through walls
as well as doors. He was so shy
he seemed pained by a greeting.
Sometimes I merely nodded,
to spare him the effort of speaking.

Until he retired at eighty-six,
Winer made classic Abaco dinghies,
simple working boats,
elegantly proportioned,
all sweet-smelling wood.

Electricity came to Hope Town,
but not to Winer.
Every inch of each boat
was done by hand
in the little shed
beside his home.

People came from far away
to buy his boats or just to watch him work.

So many stopped in Vernon's store
to ask, "Where is the boat builder?"
that Winer complained he could not work
and asked if Vernon
could forget to tell them his whereabouts.

He was the one who made the coffins
for Hope Town. There were
always two, one for any death, and
one a spare, on hand until
he made the next one.

Winer knew what was worth keeping
and what was not,
what was worth passing on.

On a bright clear day this January
he was laid to rest in the upper cemetery.

Standing at his grave for the service,
we look straight out to sea.
I like to think of Winer
in an Abaco dinghy of his own making,
under the bluest sky, with
just a breath of wind to fill the sails,
sailing off
toward, and over, the horizon.

Continental Drift

In Hope Town, I crawl into my side
of the king-sized bed
bought at the request of our renters,
who must all be giants,

and roll across deserts and seas,
mountains and meadows,
until at last I reach your side
and touch your sleeping form

with the comfort of continents
reunited 200 million years
after drifting apart.
Now the coast of Africa
tucks in alongside Brazil.
At last, Pangaea, All Earth.

In Chicago, we slept for years
in the same narrow four-poster double bed,
its size become so rare
that sheets to fit
were hard to find.

Friends who saw our bedroom wondered aloud
how my six-foot husband and I
slept in that tiny bed.
"Easily," I said. "Like spoons."

Off on 9:45 Ferry

Stripped of its sheets,
your room looks bare.
Your beach towels, still damp,
hang over the porch railing,
tumbled by an Atlantic breeze.
On the outside table,
the baby's water shoes.

Adelaide's Bracelet

For her 100th birthday

At a full moon party
at our house on the Atlantic,
we all sat outside until after dark.
Adelaide broke a silent spell,
extending her arm,
gesturing toward the silver sky and sea,
saying, "Have you ever seen anything more lovely
than that moon on the water?"

We agreed that we had not
(*although*, I thought, *Adelaide herself is lovely*).

Toward the evening's end,
Adelaide took her bracelet from her arm,
a string of silver sand dollars.
She fastened it, still warm, on my arm
where you see it now.
As she gave it to me, she said,
"So you will always have sand,
you will always have a dollar, and
you will always have me."

Bahama Wind

The wind comes up to show us who's boss.
Like a giant eggbeater, it whips
spindrift into the air.
It throws sand into my eyes and hair
like a naughty child playing on the beach.
It shreds the blue and yellow Bahamian flag,
whistles at windows and door sills.

It gets inside your head,
scrambles your dreams,
chases your thoughts around.
It grabs your words
as you speak to your friend.
You go away unheard.

At night, clouds seem to blow
across the moon's face.
I hear in the wind's moaning the voices
of those who went to sea
and did not return.

A bender, a spree:
days of roaring through town,
traipsing down the beach,
screeching in the high casuarinas.
Then like a dog getting comfortable
it turns around three times, lies down
and goes to sleep.

The Wind Blows Open the Door

In the freezing storm,
the wind blows open the door.
No one is home.
Pipes freeze and break.

A plumber is called,
but silently, in the dark,
water breaches the walls,
seeping under the rug,
buckling the floor.

Like the end of a love,
the wind blows open the door.
You see something
you've never seen before.
Walls crumble.
All else is wreckage.

Eric the Barber

Eric Auguste, called Eric the Barber
for the fine haircuts he gave,
rode out Hurricane Dorian
in Treasure Cay, Bahamas,
with his family in their small frame house.

His mother, visiting from Haiti,
chose to stay with them,
despite his pleas for her to fly out.
She said, "If you fight, I fight with you guys."

When flood waters reached their necks,
they had to swim for it
out into the storm.

Holding his mother's hand,
he swam out into the monstrous flood.
The 200 mph wind
sucked out all their breath.
They could not hear each other speak.

Those winds
drove a piece of plywood
through Eric's arm,
severing it above the elbow.

He was rescued, and he survived.
Later, from his hospital bed,
he told reporters that
as he saw his mother taken by the flood,

washed out to sea,
he could see that she was smiling.

I believe him.
I think she was saying
You tried your best. Don't worry.
I will be all right.

With a beaming, tearful face
he thanked God for that comfort,
for his life, and for the fact
that it was his left arm, not his right.
He will cut hair again.

Lost Souls

I lie, not sleeping, in my bed
listening to the rumbling of the sea,
sometimes placid, a blue mirror
for gliding boats. But
do not be deceived.
The sea is no more forgiving
than gravity is forgiving of
a man who falls from a tower
onto the rocks below.

We have heard news of people
from Haiti, thirty or so souls
(the true number we'll never know)
vanished under the waves,
boat smashed against the reef
short miles from this island,
near Fowl Cay last night.

Poor Haiti,
broken by earthquakes,
fires, cholera,
murderous misrule of
Papa Doc, Baby Doc and others,
so hopeless that
people risk life,
as others have before them,
leaving at night in a rickety boat.

Last night many died. Some
were plucked from the waves by rescuers
or saved their own lives by
swimming all the way to Scotland Cay –
only to be deported today.

Haitian Village Called "The Mud"

The flames, the chaos, the noise, the smell of smoke,
the fear.
You run and snatch what can be saved,
the baby, your other children,
leaving behind everything else not on your body:
your shoes, the children's shoes, the baby's toys,
the one surviving photo of your mother,
the backpacks packed for next morning's school day,
the hope of a better life in a new place.

Now you get up each morning,
try to find food and shelter,
calm the children –
do what can be done in one day's time.

On an island a short ferry ride away
people stuff black garbage bags
with children's clothes, tennis shoes, flip flops,
cans of food, new backpacks.

Albury's ferry brings these to you without charge,
and maybe with them a sliver of hope.

Cuba, 2011

for Sarah

The taxi is a Russian *Lada*
from the fifties.
I open the taxi door
and the handle comes off in my hand.
I set it on the seat beside me.
The driver smiles and shrugs.
It has happened before.

We enter the café.
It isn't clean
but a band is playing.
The music is good,
and a young girl plays a flute solo.
No one seems to be working here.
We find a table for four and stay.

After a long wait,
a waitress walks over,
gives us two mimeographed paper menus
for four people.
We share menus.
She mentions one dish,
the kabobs, as a special.

A half hour later, she returns.
Our daughter, in perfect Spanish,
orders for us all.
To each request,

the waitress says, *No!*
as if insulted.

We stare at each other,
silent now, uncomprehending,
unsure of what comes next.
She throws up her hands,
Esta Cuba! she says.

They are out of everything,
all of the items
on the menus we hold.

We understand.
We order kabobs for four.

Touring Cairo

I walk alongside the Nile,
a river too dirty to touch,
in Cairo, Egypt's most crowded city,
where a baby is born every 23 seconds.

I move briskly, as instructed,
through a crowd of young men
hawking trinkets, postcards.

They follow me,
holding up scarves for my choice
or flipping postcards in my face,
repeating *One dollar,*
one American dollar.

I push on through,
meeting no one's eyes,
saying *Lal, lal, lal, shokran,*
(no, no thank you)
until a child I'd refused
lowers his postcards,
catches my eye, and makes,
with his fingers bunched up near his mouth,
motions miming eating.

I empty my purse
into his outstretched hand,
not much, just a few Egyptian pounds,
and watch, ashamed, as he closes his fist and runs
off down the Corniche,
as if afraid I'd try to take it back.

In Jordan

Northwest of Madaba
Mount Nebo stands
where Moses was shown
the promised land.

He would not enter
but his people would.
Here is the spot where Moses stood.
How could he know it would end in blood?

The State of the Republic

Free press is the enemy of the state,
tweets the Manchurian candidate.

We slide deeper into the mire.
How long before our Reichstag Fire?

Anxiety morphs into fear.
Will his enemies disappear?

Achtung!
Stay awake.

The Tree of the World

for Margy Pastor

What to do if you
have a father who
cuts down the tree of the world,
who believes in the sword?

Why not then
sail to the end
of the world,
travel alone
to Easter Island,
a place without a tree,
without a stick of wood.

Why not then sit,
eyes fixed on the horizon
like the eyes of the Moai,
the great stone statues.

Can you see through
to the green core
of the tree of the world?

Despite the axe,
despite puny man,
can you see, year after year,
ring after ring,
how the sap still runs,
how the leaves unfurl?

III.

The Offering of the Lotus

for John

In the Cairo museum,
an ancient golden sculpture shows
the young pharoah's wife-to-be
anointing him with perfume,
her slender frame bent over
his seated majesty.

He wears only one sandal
of a pair, she the other,
a sign of their deep love.

She offers him a single lotus.

If he accepts it,
they will be married.

His hand is touching it.

Anniversary, Uxmal

Walking back in the rain
from the ruins at Uxmal,
gravel scratching under sandals.
Rain drips from the eaves
of my straw hat.
Altamira Oriole
sings in the coppice,
hops from a twig
to a drier branch.

Forty years ago, we stayed here,
same hacienda, perhaps same room
under the same towering trees.

In our path iguana pokes his armored head
from his hole, scans for danger.
We won't hurt him. He won't hurt us.

Though short in Mayan time,
our love feels as ancient, as timeless
as the Temple of the Magician.
Magically we build it over and over again,
stone on stone, step by step.

Something so precious could spark
jealousy in the gods. Looking to appease,
I call down protection for us both
from the Mayan gods
of earth, water, wind and fire,
from the four corners of the universe.

Somewhere the oriole is singing.
Different bird, same song.

Smoke

for John

Cold spring. Wind howls up the chimney.
We sit in rockers before our stone fireplace
reading and dozing.
Around eleven we climb the stairs to bed.
As I hold you, I find your hair smells like smoke,
just as it did in the thirty plus seasons
when we sat by a glowing campfire we had made
after a long day of whitewater canoeing,
following the v in the white water, avoiding
rocks the size of houses,
paddling until our muscles were spent
and we were wet and cold.
After an easy dinner cooked outside
we doused the fire
and climbed into our one-person orange pup tent,
our two sleeping bags
zipped together to make one.

Ultrasound

for Molly and John

Our daughter-in-law,
lithe and strong,
stretches out, stomach bared
to the wand
while we watch
patterns on a screen,
kaleidoscope of flesh
and bone, shifting, turning,
resembling nothing human.
Oh, but there, a tadpole spine,
side view of skull,
thumb reaching toward mouth.

Then, unmistakable,
a tiny heart beating,
opening, closing,
like a fist,
like wings
of a perched bird
preparing for flight.

Grandmother's Shoes

A farmer's wife,
Grandmother wore black lace-up shoes
with a wide one-inch heel.
She rushed from chore to chore
sunup to sundown
day after livelong day.

Out at sunrise for milking,
she sat on a low stool
pulling in rhythm at the cow's udder.
Fresh, sweet smelling milk,
still warm,
pinged into the bucket.
Grandmother would turn deftly,
squirt milk into the mouth
of a waiting barn cat
without missing a pull.

Off to the cellar,
she poured her buckets of milk
into the separator,
skimming the cream
to sell it separately
or putting it aside
to turn it into butter
in her wooden churn
while she sat on the porch
at day's end.

She walked the path
to the hen house,

threw out grain for the chicks,
gathered the warm eggs
from under the feathered breasts
of the clucking, pecking broody hens.

All day, my feet in flip flops,
I followed in her footsteps.
The pain in her feet
caused her clumping side-to-side gait
as she hurried from house to barn
to hen house and back to kitchen
to make bacon and flapjacks for the men.

Bewitched by a picture catalog,
she spent her egg money on
anti-arthritic shoes.

When they failed
to ease her painful feet,
she reverted to her old shoes
clomped down the cellar stairs,
offending shoes in hand,
opened the furnace door
and threw them into the fire.

At the Villa Borghese

Bernini's statue of Apollo and Dafna is
fashioned so like human flesh
that Apollo's hands, grasping the fleeing girl,
leave impressions on her marble thigh.

Her mouth is open, voicing a
scream we cannot hear.
Even her toes are flexed in terror.

The guide says: "Ever since Dafna was turned
into a laurel tree, laurel has been honored,
woven to form the victor's crown,
found in the words we use for honors,
Poet Laureate, Nobel Laureate, Baccalaureate."

I think of my patients at the shelter,
their lives changed by rape.
Damage remains, years later.

Dafna escaped the only way she could.
As we watch,
she is becoming a tree,
her hands, her fingers
turning to laurel leaves,
her hips to bark.

Her pursuer is beautiful, a god.
What surprise to him to find that she,
the human woman
he said he loved,
the one whose thigh

bears the marks of his hands,
whose tears run down
her human cheek,

has learned to become a thing,
inanimate, immovable,
sending down roots,
turning to branches,
escaping into the forest of her body.

Maya: Illusion

Four days of yoga on an island
in the Bahamas,
sweating through asanas,
four-hour sessions,
deepening, opening
heart and head chakras
finding stillness amidst chaos,
leaving illusions on the mat.

We sat in silent lotus,
next-door to casinos
where shouts and laughter
spilled from high lighted windows.

You could almost hear
click of dice
rush of slots
calls of dealers
whoops of winners
sighs of losers.

Last day,
workshop over,
two monks, holy men,
shaven heads, saffron robes,
constant smiles,
joined me on
my cab ride from the hotel
to the airport.

They asked the taxi driver
to please stop at the casino

and left the cab, bowing low,
prayer hands at hearts, "Namaste."

Seeing my surprise,
one monk turned to me, laughing,
saying, "You must swim in the Maya!"

Twenty Years Ago

Twenty years ago,
in a Quaker meeting for the purpose of marriage,
our daughter and son-in-law
sat in silence
until they were moved to rise,
face each other, and say their vows.

Melting snow dripped
into the sanctuary
from the flat church roof,
first pinging then plopping into tin buckets,
for long stretches the only sound we heard
until a guest rose to speak.

Those of us who were there
signed a document which was framed,
hanging in their hallway since that day,
swearing our intent to uphold
their choice of each other.

Years later
two children came to them from China.
They held them joyfully,
marveling at each new word and step.

Now he has moved out.

Alone, she readies the girls for school.
Two lunches for tomorrow are packed,
waiting in the refrigerator.

Mornings she writes for pay.
Afternoons she walks the dog along the lakeshore.

There is a blankness on the wall
where the document had been.
Paint there is darker. It never faded.

Preparing the Roses for Winter

for John

The roses underperformed this year,
even the red Knockouts and climbing pinks.
Despite my weeding,
talking to them,
they've suffered from mildew,
black spot, Japanese beetles.
Maybe the words I thought talismanic
were only words.

I cut them back hard
and throw the prickly branches
into the compost.

I confide in my husband
my despair
as we move together
working side by side.
I say I should give up on them and
plant prairie grasses, something invincible.
He says, "You've never
given up on anything yet."

I stop work for the moment,
chilled, exhausted,
tending the thorn embedded in my finger
and the one embedded in my heart,
worry over one of our grown children.

How did I dream

that our love would
nurture our children
beyond sorrow,
shelter them from grief?

My husband gardens
well into the November dark,
first laying newspaper
then heaping mulch in a protective layer
over the roots of each rose,
troweling in delicate daubs,
the last of our compost.

When he finishes
his jacket is filthy,
beyond cleaning.

It's dirty work,
the work of love.

Dismantling the Fairy House

for Maya

Maya made a house for fairies.
The sign over the door says *Welcome Fairies!*
I gave her my small earring boxes
which became fairy beds,
three of them with cotton batting coverlets
labeled *fairy beds* so there would be no mistake.
There is a couch, also labeled
and softened with cotton batting.
Taped to the walls,
there are small flowers, now dried,
bougainvillea and a lily,
because fairies love flowers.

I must put it away now.
Soon we leave our own fairy house.
I haven't seen fairies there, but
they may come out at night.
They are evanescent, like fireflies,
like five-year-old girls.
I hope they find a new home.

Let Morning Come

Homage to Jane Kenyon

Let the first light spread gold through the clouds
over a purple sea.
Let the waves comb the hair of the sea oats.
Let the breeze rise and
ruffle the curtain by the east window.
Let the soft light move slowly
up the wall, touching
the Sunrise Tellins in their glass bowl.
Let morning come.

Let the night's dew dry off.
Somewhere on the island
let a rooster crow.
Let the night's dreams slip away.
Let the heart give over its grieving.
Let morning come.

Let the sleeper awake and
turn to his lover.
Let the coffee leap and boil in the pot.
Let the lighthouse put away its light
until tonight.
This is the day that the Lord has made,
so let morning come.

Sweet Light

Sweet Light is what
photographers call
the last few moments before sunset.
Shots taken then
are sweet as the seed
of the pomegranate,
as the heart of the watermelon.

We treasure that half hour in Hope Town
when all things under the sun
seem burnished, golden.
Babies look like cherubim.
The aged appear gracious, wise,
their eyes wreathed in wrinkles.

We raise a toast to each other
in that sweet light.

Seeing

The only reason to be an artist is to find a new way of seeing.
                                  – Morandi

Our teacher tells us:
We paint to see what we are seeing.
Have no preconceived ideas.

Start with a line, vertical or horizontal.
Follow the line across the page –
don't stop.
A line has tension and movement.
Take the direction that seems wrong to you.

Get your shapes in first.
Put in dark shapes until the light shapes have meaning.
Paint shapes, not objects.

Find the light in your picture.
Find where the light strikes.
Work toward the light.
Paint the color of the light as
it hits the object.

The color you put down
helps you find the next color.
Color changes each instant, so
just paint a piece of it.
Paint what you see at that moment.
The viewer's eye follows
the rhythm of the painter's eye.
It is a dance between the eye, the object,
the hand, the brush.

Green is a middle color, difficult to handle,
with yellow and orange moving toward you,
blue and violet falling away.
Kandinsky said: "Green is wearisome."
Sargent avoided green,
used black
to paint green pines.
We see a color by seeing
the color next to it.
Thus, orange makes blue pop.
Yellow makes violet pop.

In painting, there are moments of seeing,
moments of discovery.
Focus on deep space.
The unconscious loves deep space.

Leonardo said, "It is the invisible
that needs to be found,
not the visible."

In Between

One day, when I was twenty,
I lay on my back in the grass,
hands clasped behind my head,
watching cumulus clouds
roll in before a storm.
I remember
that moment, the
slant of light, the
prickle of grass against my skin,
its new-mown smell.

Now, fifty some odd years later,
I lie in a hammock,
watch cirrus clouds,
mare's tails, scudding
across a cerulean sky.
I half listen to the sea,
to the click of palm leaves.
I feel the breeze on my skin.

What happened in between?
I was busy,
living my one and only life.
Moments of joy, like this one,
remain
outside of time.

Felucca

Let me drift on a slow felucca
down the wide and moveless Nile,
where palm trees line the shore,
distant hills show green, then brown,
where papyrus on small islands
grows wild.

Let me float on a slow felucca
with a man at the stern
whose language is as strange to me
as mine to him,
a man in a gray *galabaya*
and a white head wrap
to shelter him
from a sun gone mad.

Let me sail in a felucca
where nothing seems to move,
not the sun,
not the river, not the man,
only my gaze
and the boat under sail.

Advice

Swing open the skylights.
Hot days, dark nights,
lightning over the lake,
rain on the wind, then a gusher
sluices down the old drain pipe.
The door to the garden stands open.
Walk through it
into the scent of verbena.

Let the weeds take your garden,
start again next year.
Plant more herbs.
Drink wine while cooking,
turn up the music until
pots vibrate on the stove.

But let not all dear words be lost.
Turn them into song
and whisper even
into the ear of death.

Sit with me here in the sun
on the hillside this morning.
Take grief under your wing.

Stroke it, soothe it,
comfort it.
Watch the way the leaves
of the alder turn themselves
silver side up in the breeze.

ABOUT THE AUTHOR

A nn Marie Gearen is a retired psychotherapist who worked for twenty-five years at a shelter for women and children affected by domestic violence. She holds a doctorate in English literature and a masters in social work. With her husband, she lives in Oak Park, Illinois, and Hope Town, Abaco, Bahamas, where a beloved community is still recovering from the disaster of Hurricane Dorian. Her first poetry collection is *Homecoming* (2007). Her work has appeared in *Primavera, After Hours, Calyx, Abaco Life*, and *River Oak Arts*, where her poem "Homecoming" was a prize-winner.

T his book is set in Garamond Premier Pro, which had its genesis in
1988 when type-designer Robert Slimbach visited the Plantin-
Moretus Museum in Antwerp, Belgium, to study its collection of
Claude Garamond's metal punches and typefaces. During the mid-
fifteen hundreds, Garamond—a Parisian punch-cutter—produced a
refined array of book types that combined an unprecedented degree of
balance and elegance, for centuries standing as the pinnacle of beauty
and practicality in type-founding. Slimbach has created an entirely new
interpretation based on Garamond's designs and on compatible italics
cut by Robert Granjon, Garamond's contemporary.

For more concerning the work of Ann Gearen,
visit www.antrimhousebooks.com/authors.html.

This book is available at all bookstores
including Amazon, or you can order
directly from the author:

Ann M. Gearen
721 Ontario St., Apt. 206
Oak Park, IL 60302
jgearen@yahoo.com.
Send $17 per book
(checks payable to Ann M. Gearen)
plus $3 for shipping.